How to Write Ethics Essays

Peter Baron

Published by Inducit Learning Ltd trading as pushmepress.com,

Mid Somerset House, Southover, Wells

Somerset BA5 1UH, United Kingdom

www.pushmepress.com

First published in 2014

ISBN: 978-1-909618-97-8

Contents

PRACTICAL ESSAY EXAMPLES

1. "Kantian ethics is the best approach to issues surrounding abortion." Discuss.

2. "Free will is incompatible with determinism." Discuss.

3. Assess which theory of utilitarianism gives the best account of moral decision-making.

4. Distinguish between absolute and relativist morality.

5. "Moral statements are merely an expression of feeling." Discuss.

6. "Ayer's verification principle is meaningless." Discuss.

7. Explain the main principles of Classical Utilitarianism.

8. Explain how a follower of Kantian ethics might approach the issues surrounding the right to child.

9. "Conscience is the voice of God." Discuss.

10. Opening paragraphs - five examples of good practice.

Foreword

This book is written by an experienced Religious Studies teacher who has spent his whole academic life doing moral philosophy, first at Oxford University, and then in the classroom with generations of highly stimulating students.

The book is unique in this sense, that throughout the book I use practical examples from students writing under exam conditions in an exam hall. There is nothing fake about the marks they are awarded.

What I have tried to do is to extract some key principles of essay-writing in a highly analytical style, in a subject that involves complex issues. Trite answers, unclear reasoning, over-generalisation have no place in philosophy essays.

As well as a contents index, there is an index of practical examples with the actual essay titles used.

I have tried to range fairly widely across the AS and A2 Ethics syllabus and provided strong as well as weak examples.

Further examples can be found on our website which is continually updated. See the final chapter on getting more help.

This book is dedicated to our students over the years who have given us so much stimulating food for thought.

The Nature of an Ethics Essay

Ethics essays (Moral Philosophy) are essays of a certain sort unique to this subject. This is because they involve construction and evaluation of arguments, and because their style is characterised by great clarity and relevance.

An argument is not an opinion. An opinion says "I prefer tea to coffee," or "I think Mill's view of utilitarianism is superior to Bentham's." Whereas an argument justifies this **ASSERTION** by careful consideration of different positions - "Mill's rule utilitarianism presents a case for justice and minority rights based on a general sympathy which elevates it above the hedonism of Bentham."

An argument is not a feeling. Arguments proceed by reasoning, so there is such a thing as a false move or **FALLACY** in an argument. It is the nature of sound arguments that the conclusion must follow from what you have said, after carefully weighing **ALTERNATIVE VIEWPOINTS**.

Above all, ethics essays are characterised by **LOGICAL ANALYSIS**. In the sections that follow we explore and then apply principles of how to write logically and analytically.

Constructing the Essay

INTRODUCTIONS AND CONCLUSIONS

An ethics essay has a main point or **THESIS**. A thesis is one sentence which sums up what you are trying to establish as your conclusion.

When you are faced with an essay title, practise constructing your thesis in one sentence. This thesis will then appear in your introduction (see below for how this can thesis statement can be introduced).

Practical example 1

> *"Kantian ethics is the best approach to issues surrounding abortion." Discuss.*

Thesis: Kantian ethics is incapable of considering the complexities of individual ethical dilemmas as it is based on absolutes derived from the categorical imperative.

This thesis is clear, brief, and relevant to the question set. I am not trying to prove the thesis here, that will form the substance of my essay, but I am stating it so the reader is completely clear as to what that thesis is.

Sometimes we may be unsure of what line to take on an essay title. If we are unsure we need to adopt a different approach - to ask questions about the question. In this example I am going to show you how we can present a line on a question through the tactic of interrogating the question before we start.

Practical example 2: A different approach to the thesis

▸ **"Assess which theory of utilitarianism gives the best account of moral decision-making".**

Here are three questions (of many) we might ask about this question.

1. How does utilitarianism arrive at a meaning of the good?

2. Which of the three utilitarian theories presents the most practical account when the meaning is applied to a situation?

3. What do we mean by "best" in the sense of moral decision-making?

We then have a tailor-made paragraph structure.

- **PARAGRAPH 1** - Utilitarianism arrives at goodness by assuming one intrinsic good, happiness or pleasure, and then arguing for an empirical calculation of the balance of pleasure or happiness over pain. It is a scientific approach which has the benefit that everyone is treated as equal, and the thing maximised is supposedly easy to calculate.

- **PARAGRAPHS 2 AND 3** - Bentham's account is hedonic as it is based on the idea of measuring pleasure in hedons. This is difficult to do in practice as there is no clear indication that my hedon value equals yours - for instance, I award a mars bar three hedons and you award it four. Also the idea of maximising utility doesn't account for the problem of average utility, as an average may rise when one person is given a huge increase in pleasure. There is generally a problem of distribution of utilitarian ethics. Mill tried to escape this problem by arguing for justice in distribution of benefits and equal rights. But his compromise may not work because he himself allows us to break a rule if there is a clear utilitarian case.

- **PARAGRAPH 4** - In contrast, Peter Singer's utilitarian ethic rests on the maximising of first choices. This is a simple vote on a stated preference, we are not asked to weigh hedons and add them up. The student could explain how this works and then come to a decision as to which is superior as an approach. But the conclusion here unfolds as part of the analysis.

An alternative suggested earlier is that we work out our thesis in advance and then state it straightaway in the introductory paragraph. The thesis is then restated at the end, with additions and qualifications judged relevant from the whole essay. The thesis doesn't have to be the very first sentence, but here I will make it the first sentence.

> *"I will argue that Mill's utilitarianism, with its emphasis on social rules and higher and lower pleasures, is superior to Bentham's act utilitarianism and Singer's preference utilitarianism as it protects individual rights and places justice as the prime concern of utilitarian ethics. By contrast, Singer places too much emphasis on rational choice, thereby devaluing the sanctity of*

life of the unborn and the newborn up to eight-weeks-old.
Bentham, in addition, places over-reliance on an empirical
measurement of pleasure and wrongly argues that pleasure is
the supreme good".

This is the position I am seeking to defend which will be worked out in the bulk of the essay. Notice that no examiner can accuse me of not answering the question, and as long as I keep disciplined in my thought process, I simply amplify the thesis stated at the beginning of my essay and restate it as a conclusion. I could equally well have preferred Bentham's utilitarianism or Singer's: I would have marshalled my argument a different way but the technique of producing an argument justified and illustrated appropriately remains identical.

THE MAIN ARGUMENT

My conclusion about Kantian ethics needs to follow from the argument that I have constructed. One way of making sure this happens is to put the thesis as the conclusion of a set of **PREMISES** or starting points - assertions I am prepared to justify in my essay as the paragraphs unfold. In my simple example below I have two premises.

- **PREMISE 1** - Kantian ethics is the ethics of universal duties established by universalising your behaviour by an a priori method.

- **PREMISE 2** - An a priori method cannot consider individual circumstances as it is a form of abstract, generalised reasoning using the imagination.

- **CONCLUSION** - Therefore Kantian ethics is unable to treat abortion on a case-by-case basis necessary to be of use to the individual facing moral dilemmas.

Another example of an argument that moves from premises to conclusion is the **ONTOLOGICAL ARGUMENT** for the existence of God. This argument is an a priori deductive argument (meaning one that moves from premises to conclusion by logic rather than appeal to facts).

- **PREMISE 1** - God is a being greater than which no being can be conceived.

- **PREMISE 2** - Even the atheist has an idea of God in his head.

- **PREMISE 3** - It is greater for something to exist in reality and the mind than it is to exist in the mind alone.

- **PREMISE 4** - If God exists in the mind alone, this contradicts our definition of God, because it would be possible for something greater than God to exist.

- **CONCLUSION** - Therefore a being called God must exist.

One possible structure for an essay on the ontological argument is to examine and then evaluate these premises one by one.

For example, look at premise one: that God is a being greater than which no being can be conceived. If we consider the Christian view of God, then it could be argued that God has moral flaws: he is angry; jealous of rivals; judges people and sentences some to hell. In this case we can argue the premise is false as we can conceive of a greater God.

In addition, the argument is often criticised as committing a bare assertion fallacy, as it offers no supportive premise other than qualities inherent in the unproven statement of premise one. This is also called a circular argument, because the premise relies on the conclusion, which in turn relies on the premise.

Whatever statements (premises) you can think of to support a conclusion (thesis), the paragraph structure can explore the outline argument structure stage-by-stage. This ensures that your analysis proceeds logically and clearly.

WORLDVIEWS

Sometimes, it is necessary to examine the worldview of an author to make the premises explicit or to find the missing premise. The worldview is often governed by culturally specific assumptions the author makes. Taking our major ethical theories as an example, here is a summary of the major worldviews and the assumptions they make. If you disagree with the assumption, and can establish it as questionable or even false, you destroy the argument. The table opposite identifies some features of the worldview underlying major ethical theories.

THEORY	ASSUMPTIONS	OBJECTIONS
Relativism	There is no universal truth	May be empirically false
Natural law	Humans by nature do good	Humans by nature are selfish and do more evil than good
Kantian ethics	Reason is divided between the noumenal and phenomenal realms, and morality belongs to the noumenal.	Moral principles seem to be derived by many philosophers from the natural or empirical world eg by adding up happiness.
Utilitarianism - Bentham	Pleasure is the only good. We can measure pleasure.	There seem to be other "goods" such as duty. We can't measure pleasure in hedons or anything else.

Divine Command	God's word is clear and unambiguous on practical issues.	Ancient texts were written from one cultural perspective which often does not address our culture directly.
Utilitarianism - Mill	There are higher and lower pleasures Rules are needed to maximise utility	This is a difficult distinction to make without sounding snobbish. Rules imply universal application - so when can you break them?
Virtue ethics	A virtue is an agreed character trait. This trait comes from the rational purpose (telos) of human beings.	We cannot agree on whether things like courage are really a moral virtue. What about the kamikaze pilot?

The above table can be added to. The idea is to expose the assumptions within the premises of an argument, as the easiest way to expose an argument as false is to expose the premise as false - or based on a faulty assumption.

SEQUENCING THOUGHT

An argument proceeds by a sequence of thought where one idea follows clearly from another. This means it is essential you construct an outline before you start to write. One way of ensuring the argument is sequential (rather than a jumbled up series of loosely related points) is to use link phrases. Here is a list.

- I will begin by ...

- The argument of this essay is that ...

- Here we need to consider the following objection ...

- In the next paragraph, I consider ...

- Having argued that X, I now wish to consider Y.

- Although I have shown X, I still need to establish Y.

- Some might object that ...

- Further support for this claim comes from W's argument.

Notice that a number of these use the personal pronoun "I". This is deliberate, as a philosophy essay is my own analysis of a question. I need to form a clear conclusion - which is my own view, fully justified, and therefore the use of "I" (unlike in other subjects) is to be encouraged.

If you want to use analytical words, here's another list. Some of these are **DEVELOPING** the argument in one line or direction, and others are **CONTRASTING** another argument with your previous line of argument:

- However

- Because (insert name of philosopher) argues this ...

- It could be argued therefore

- With regard to this

- On the other hand

- It follows from this

- It can thus be seen that

- Alternatively

- Moreover

- Furthermore

- In addition to this

- Subsequently

- Consequently

- As a result

- This would suggest

- Such an argument leads

- Kant's (or another philosopher) argument might work if ... , however,

- Aquinas (or another philosopher) is wrong however, because (we can say a philosopher is wrong, but need to say why and show how).

Practical example 3

Here is an example of an essay written in the A2 exam which gained full marks. I have added some comments.

▸ **"Free will is incompatible with Determinism." Discuss.**

To assess the extent to which free will is compatible with Determinism, one must first consider other approaches to the concept of free will and whether we, in fact, possess it. A Hard Determinist, such as Honderich, would claim that individuals are not free to initiate actions or make moral decisions, thereby making the concept of moral responsibility redundant. Any moral decisions we make have uncontrollable prior causes. Thus, a Hard Determinist would support the premise that free will and Determinism are not compatible with one another. Diametrically opposed to Hard Determinism is Libertarianism, with which free will is closely compatible. Proponents of this position, such as Kant, maintain that we are all free and should, therefore, take full moral responsibility for our actions. Between these two extremes stands Compatibilism. Classical Compatibilists, such as Hume, state that most moral decisions are the result of both external determined forces and an internal act of volition or will. In fact, they go so far as to say that true freedom requires causation, without which there would be randomness. Undeniably then, the idea of free will is incompatible with Hard Determinism. A Compatibilist or Soft Determinist, however, would refute the claim that the two concepts are incompatible. Arguably then, Libertarianism would seem to present the most

*convincing approach to the issue of free will, in that it
acknowledges the role of the individual in moral decision making
because of their free will, while accepting that the person's
background will, in part, influence the choices they make.*

Here the student uses technical language correctly, drops some names in
and also gives her essay a good twist - meaning, we know the line she's
going to take and we also see she understands precisely what issues
underlie the essay question. One technique to practise is to revise a topic
in class for example, with a powerpoint and then make up a question
with the word discuss at the end. Bring some highlighter pens in, then
peer mark highlighting where the twist occurs in the opening paragraph.
When you get bored with that, do the same with conclusions. Mark out
of ten and read them out to discuss.

*Hard Determinism holds that we do not have free will and that
all seemingly 'moral' actions are the consequences of prior
events that are out of our control. The incompatibility between
this position and freedom results in the assumption that it is
unreasonable to hold people responsible for what they do,
making praise and blame redundant. Certainly, if no-one is free
to do otherwise than they in fact do, it does seem unfair to
punish bad actions while rewarding good ones. Furthermore,
Science has proved that the world is governed by cause and
effect. For a Hard Determinist, human beings are the same as
material things, in that they are controlled by the same laws of
nature. Our wills, which we believe to be freely gained, are
actually the result of a causal chain stretching back into
childhood. The fact we are governed by our genes and our
environment means that our ability to make moral decisions as*

free agents, is illusory. As such, the Hard Determinist position seems to be incompatible with the concept of free will.

Yes, it is the scientific world view which lies at the heart of the determinist view. Recently I heard a scientist say "the brain is like a computer." My own view is that this analogy is highly misleading. Where exactly is the computer screen in your brain? It's not a very helpful analogy - and we find ourselves back with metaphysics.

This incompatibility is further demonstrated by Locke's analogy of the locked room, in which he describes a man asleep in a locked room, who, when he awakes, decides to stay there. Although he believes he is using his free will to make this decision, in reality, he could not have done otherwise - "he has not the freedom to be gone." Such an analogy underpins Locke's viewpoint that "liberty is not an idea belonging to volition," making free will "power of doing." Real freedom is more than simply feeling free; we must be able to act on our choices.

Absolutely correct - and a good way to use an argument from analogy.

Moreover, Honderich, in his rejection of free will as illusory, highlights the incompatibility between the Hard Determinist position and the concept of free will. He claims that we must give up all hope of an individual's ability to originate action, and abandon all hope of determining the future: "there can be no such hope if all the future is just an effect of effects." An implication of this is that criminals should not be punished for the crimes they commit, as they do not possess free will and,

*therefore, are not morally responsible for their actions. Although
Hard Determinists are not in favour of restorative or retributive
justice, they do accept that criminals need to be imprisoned to
protect society. Clearly then, this incompatibility between Hard
Determinism, free will and moral responsibility impacts upon our
notion of punishment. If all our actions are determined, and
murderers only murder because of faulty genes and poor
upbringing, then Hard Determinism takes away our ability to
think rationally.*

There is a good use of quotes here. It's important to bounce off actual
quotes in your thinking - if you're ever stuck on how to launch an essay,
my advice would be launch it with a quote. Notice the contrasting word
- moreover, and the link phrase "an implication of this."

*In fact, the American attorney, Clarence Darrow, used this
incompatibility as the basis of his defence of two boys charged
with the murder of 14-year-old Bobby Franks. The murderers
were both highly intelligent and had carefully planned the attack
in order to assert their superior position within society. Although
they initially faced the death penalty, Darrow managed to have
their sentence reduced to life imprisonment, arguing that the
boys were the unavoidable products of their upbringings. While
accepting that they should be imprisoned to stop them from
committing similar crimes, Darrow claimed that the boys did not
possess free will and, therefore, could not be held morally
responsible for their atrocious behaviour. Such an example
undeniably reinforces the incompatibility between Hard
Determinism and the concept of free will.*

Here the student uses examples to illustrate the points - good. The repetition of the word "therefore" throughout the essay suggests that points are being properly developed.

> *However, Hard Determinism, in its denial of the existence of free will, does not explain our behaviour of praising and blaming. We naturally feel compelled to attribute moral responsibility to others, perhaps indicating that we do, in fact, possess free will and must accept moral responsibility for our actions. There is, in addition, the problem of the consequence argument, which states that the laws of nature are not up to us: "our actions are not more than effects of other equally necessitated events." Hard Determinism undeniably puts doubt in our hopes and fears for the future, affecting the way we consider the morality of others. Such problems associated with the incompatibility between free will and Hard Determinism does, arguably, seem to limit its effectiveness when considering the issues of freedom and moral responsibility.*

This last sentence needs rephrasing. No-one is asking Hard Determinism to be effective - the issue is, is it a valid description of volition? Of course, it does have implications for punishment and responsibility - which is, perhaps, her point.

> *By contrast, the Libertarianism position is closely compatible with free will. It's more than compatible - Kant makes it a central assumption of his ethics, what he calls autonomy (freedom with reason), maintaining that we are all free and, therefore, morally responsible for our actions. Moral decisions are not random, but the result of the values and character of the*

individual. Kant, for example, stated that freedom is a necessary pre-condition for all morality. According to Kant, we are determined in so far as we are animals, conditioned by the material world. However, true freedom lies beyond this, in the noumenal realm of categories, concepts, reason and ideas. We are right to blame people for acting badly, as they have failed to employ reason, which "could have and ought to have determined the conduct of the person to be other than it is." Giving in to desires is a denial of our ability to use reason, which is essential to our humanity. For Kant, although we are influenced by our background, we are by no means wholly determined by it. Humans are free, making them the originating causes of their actions, for which they must take full moral responsibility. It is then, this close compatibility between Libertarianism and free will that leads proponents of this position to argue that freedom is necessary in understanding morality and attributing praise and blame.

Without understanding the noumenal you can't understand Kant - who centres his theory on the idea of a world behind the world of the senses. Of course, the noumenal is (by definition) not the realm of scientific cause and effect. But Kant needs careful treatment as in fact he's a Compatibilist.

The fact we all experience freedom and know what it is to resist temptation is a notable strength of Libertarianism. Similarly, the fact we are not just physical matter, but have a soul or spiritual dimension, would seem to indicate that we do, in fact, possess free will, and should, therefore, take moral responsibility for what we do.

This word "fact" is rather a strange word to use for a highly debatable concept - is there any evidence we have souls? I would have brought in the validity of metaphysics as an explanation of reality here (some things will never be reducible to scientific ideas eg love), rather than an alleged fact of the soul.

Furthermore, one could argue that the fact we all make conscious ethical choices, is proof that we are not determined, but autonomous moral agents. Equally, however, a Hard Determinist could refute this claim by stating that, just because we think we have free will, doesn't mean that we actually do. We may believe we are deliberating over a moral decision, when, in reality, the choice we finally make is the inevitable result of background causes. This argument was outlined by Spinoza in Ethics.

Classical Compatibilism, standing between Hard Determinism and Libertarianism, is, to a certain extent, compatible with the concept of free will. It states that human freedom cannot be understood without Hard Determinism, as choice is one of the causal factors and has to, itself, be caused by a determinant. Most human choices then, are a combination of two factors: volition or will and external factors. Without Hard Determinism, the will would be uncaused, resulting in randomness. Humans are both free and determined, and these concepts are compatible. A Compatibilist would argue, therefore, that, while we do possess moral responsibility, it is inevitably determined by an individual's background, genetics and education. Hume, a key proponent of Classical Compatibilism, produces, in An Enquiry Concerning Human Understanding, a psychological argument, claiming that there is a psychological link between motives and resulting actions. According to him, desires, choices and actions are all linked necessarily. Although we do act according to our free will, we do not originate acts. Because of his belief that, without causation there would be randomness, Hume acknowledges that Determinism is, to a certain extent, true, meaning that we are not fully free and do not, therefore, have full moral responsibility.

However, Hume does deny that causes and effects are linked necessarily, stating that, although we experience them as linked, there is no clear basis for claiming that a cause results in an effect. So, while being a Compatibilist, Hume was also sceptical about causation and the issue of whether we have free will and moral responsibility, thereby limiting the credibility of his theory. Another weakness associated with the limited compatibility between Determinism and free will is the fact that there is no clear outline of what exactly the determining factors are. Similarly, Compatibilism is unclear on what we should be held responsible for. Moreover, a Libertarian could criticise the position for its failure to realise the extent of our free will, while a Determinist could do likewise for its inability to realise the extent to which our free will is limited.

Good essays force the teacher to go back and re-read original sources - which is what I need to do to check whether this is a correct reading of Hume. Hume argues free will requires necessity (his word for determinism).

Contemporary Compatibilists, such as Kane and Vardy, adapted the Classical Compatibilist position. Kane, for example, in An Introduction to Free Will, outlines five freedoms: self realisation, rational self control, self perfection, self determination and self formation. It is self formation that establishes a sense of free will and moral responsibility, and allows us to act in a way not determined by our pre-existing character, allowing us to make the choice to change. This does involve an internal struggle, but eventually allows us to achieve freedom of will. Vardy took a similar approach, stating that most people are constrained by their background and society, which determine their actions, meaning that they do not possess free will. However, Vardy did claim that it is possible, through hardship and struggle, to attain this freedom. In order to do this, it is necessary to understand the effects our genetic dispositions inevitably have on our tendencies, thereby coming to terms with the effects of our parents, childhood and education on our hopes, fears and expectations: "wisdom and freedom are closely linked." This approach, which stresses the limited compatibility between Determinism and free will, could be linked to Plato's analogy of the cave, in which it is the philosopher's task to seek release from the shadows of this world and achieve freedom and clarity.

Arguably then, Hard Determinism does not, in its claim that we are not morally responsible for our actions, provide a satisfactory response to the issues of freedom and morality. As such, it is most certainly incompatible with free will. Moreover, it cannot, ultimately, be proven. As such, Libertarianism, with which free will is closely compatible, would seem to provide the most *appealing approach, in that it distinguishes between personality, which is determined by the phenomenal world, and the moral self, through which we experience freedom through acts of will and for which we are all individually responsible.*

This student might have said a bit more about Kant - but on the other hand the essay is on the long side anyway. I think you can see it is very well structured and goes to the heart of the issues - concluding clearly and strongly - full marks.

Introductions and Conclusions

How you start an essay will define how successful it is as an answer to a question. The problem we face is that not all questions are clear or at least,they may not be clear to me. So we need to adopt one of two approaches. If the question is clear, then I need to present my thesis as soon as possible and make it absolutely clear what my thesis is, then the introductory paragraph and the conclusion wil relate to one another because the conclusion is the thesis explained and restated in summary. However, it will sometimes be the case that the question is unclear, or unclear to me. A strong candidate will adopt the tactic of imposing a line on the question which makes sense and is a perfectly valid intepretation of it. I call this tactic, asking questions about the question and demonstrate in practical example two (above), how this approach can be used to impose a very successful line on a question that may not be crystal clear to me.

It is a useful exercise to re-write the opening paragraphs of essays which don't score an A grade at the first attempt.

Practical example 4: strong and weak introductions and conclusions

▸ **"Distinguish between absolute and relative morality."**

> *"With ethics, morality can be either absolute or relative. It cannot be both, however, many religious ethics may have part of their ethics as relative and part as absolute."*

This is a weak opening for two reasons. First, it doesn't say anything substantial. Why not define the two terms or present a contrast between them? Secondly, it manages to contradict itself. The essay says first, that theories cannot contain elements of both and then, that theories do contain elements of both. In an actual OCR AS exam this essay scored 13/25.

Notice that in AS questions we are only asked to do a part of an essay. Part a answers should take 30 minutes, and are descriptive in nature rather than evaluative.

You are never expected to evaluate in part a AS questions.

Hence it is important to launch straight into your answer without too much introductory material. So it's often best to begin with a definition of the key terms - in this case the words "absolute" and "relative", and your thesis could be to explain the ambiguities in each term (for example, absolute can mean *universal*, or *having no exceptions*, or *objective*), and then apply them to a specific example.

- **"Explain the concept of relativist morality." (AS OCR June 2009**

> *"A moral relativist would question 'what do we mean by good?' when deliberating the best, most moral action to take when faced with an ethical decision. An example of a relativist moral statement is: 'I ought not to steal because I will cause suffering to those I steal from.' This is a reasonable statement, considering the consequences of a potential action. It is teleological, in that it is concerned with ends (Greek word 'telos' meaning end or purpose). Relativism is in direct contrast with absolute morality which is deontological and concerned with the actions themselves. A moral relativist would not believe that there is a fixed set of moral rules that apply to all people all times, in all places. Rather, they would leave the morality is changeable and differs culture-to-culture, time-to-time, and place-to-place. This idea is known as cultural relativism."*

This paragraph successfully launches the answer by making a clear distinction between absolute and relative morality, defining the terms, and going straight to the heart of the difference between the two concepts. Although the word "absolute" is not contained in the title, it is always a good tactic to set up a contrast between two ideas, such that the differences between them highlight the essential nature of relativism. The key contrast is set up with the link word "rather." The essay scored 25/25.

COMMAND WORDS

COMMAND WORDS - are words in the title which require a certain line of analysis or evaluation. What is the difference between the two concepts?

ANALYSIS - provides the reasons that establish a conclusion. In other words, the analysis supports the conclusion.

Imagine I am given a car to test. On one level I can analyse how it works. I can look at the engine design and the number of seats, the aerodynamics. I can explain the linkages between wheels and engine, the power-to-weight ratio, the acceleration.

Then, I can move on to **EVALUATE** the car. I can do this in two ways.

1. I can compare the car with another to see which is **BETTER**. So I can do the same in Philosophy, by comparing Kantian ethics with Utilitarian ethics, for example - which gives the better account of morality (of course, "better' here needs definition). Do I mean, more easy to apply, more understandable, or more realistic in light of human psychology?). If we are not being asked to evaluate, then we shouldn't really be presenting such a contrast.

2. I can evaluate the car against some **OBJECTIVE** standard. For example, there may be objective measures of how a car handles, such as the famous Elk test in Sweden by which a car is braked very hard on an icy road to see if it turns over. One famous make of car did turn over, to the embarrassment of the manufacturer! We may do the same in Philosophy. There are objective tests for the logic of arguments - as the chapter on fallacies explains.

Here, then are the main command words (words in the title).

- **ACCOUNT FOR** - requires an answer that gives the reasons for the subject of the question.

- **ANALYSE** - requires an answer that takes apart an idea, concept or statement in order to consider all the factors it consists of. Answers of this type should be very methodical and logically organised.

- **ASSESS** - requires weighing an argument to consider its main features, and the strengths and weaknesses of elements of the argument.

- **COMPARE** - requires an answer that sets items side-by-side and shows their similarities and differences. A balanced (fair, objective) answer is expected.

- **CONSIDER** - requires an answer in which the students describe and give their thoughts on the subject.

- **CONTRAST** - requires an answer that points out only the differences between two ideas or theories.

- **CRITICISE** - requires an answer that points out mistakes or weaknesses, and that also indicates any favourable aspects of the subject of the question. It requires a balanced answer.

- **DEFINE** - requires an answer that explains the precise meaning of a concept.

- **DESCRIBE** - requires an answer that says what something is like, how it works and what is essential features are.

- **DISCUSS** - requires an answer that explains an idea or concept, and then gives details about it with supportive information, examples, points for and against, and explanations for the facts put forward. It is important to give both sides of an argument and come to a conclusion.

- **ELUCIDATE** - requires an answer that explains what something means, makes it clear (lucid).

- **EVALUATE** - require an answer that decides and explains how great, valuable or important something is. The judgement should be backed by a discussion of the evidence or reasoning involved.

- **EXPLAIN** - requires an answer that offers a rather detailed and exact explanation of an idea or principle, or a set of reasons for a situation or attitude.

- **EXPLORE** - requires an answer that examines the subject thoroughly and considers it from a variety of viewpoints.

- **ILLUSTRATE** - requires an answer that consists mainly of examples to demonstrate or prove the subject of the question. It is often added to another instruction.

- **JUSTIFY** - requires an answer that gives only the reasons for a position or argument. Answer the main objections likely to be made of them. Note, however, that the proposition to be argued may be a negative one (e.g. Justify the abolition of the death penalty. Prove/Disprove.) Both of these require answers that demonstrate the logical arguments and/or evidence connected with a proposition; prove requires the "pro" points, and disprove requires the "contra" points.

- **STATE** - requires an answer that expresses the relevant points briefly and clearly without lengthy discussion or minor details.

- **SUMMARISE/OUTLINE** - requires an answer that contains a summary of all the available information about a subject, i.e. only the main points and not the details should be included. Questions of this type often require short answers.

- **TRACE** - is found most frequently in historical questions (but not only in History courses); it requires the statement and brief description in logical or chronological order of the stages (steps) in the development of, for example, a theory, a person's life, a process, etc.

- **TO WHAT EXTENT IS X TRUE?** - requires an answer that discusses and explains in what ways X is true and in what ways X is not true.

THE CONCLUSION

Using the same two essays on relativism in example 4, we can clearly see the difference between a strong and weak conclusion.

Essay 1

> "In conclusion, both relative and absolute morality have many pros and cons. Neither one is better than the other, because they are extremely different."

What is wrong with this conclusion? First of all, the student was asked to distinguish between absolute and relative morality, not evaluate the two (which means compare and say which is stronger or weaker as a theory of ethics). Secondly, the student doesn't present a clear, reasoned opinion. To say "there are pros and cons for each theory" doesn't tell us what they are, nor does it suggest any implications - even if this point were relevant (which it isn't, as it is evaluating not distinguishing). The analysis here should have been by way of **CONTRAST** between the two, and the conclusion should have reworked the contrast.

Essay 2

> "An example of changing morality between cultures is infanticide which was practised by the Greeks and Romans. Everyone in our modern society considers this completely wrong and immoral. However, for them, there was no problem with it. It was socially accepted. Similarly, in Islamic cultures, many of the women choose to wear head scarves as a mark of their faith.

Many people in all other cultures see this to be unfair and restricting, a way of taking away the woman's rights to be individual. <u>However</u> the woman make the choice to do it because in their culture and their mind, it is considered morally acceptable and common practice. Advocates of moral relativism see the diverse nature of our world and the existence of many different ethical viewpoints as proof that no moral absolutes exist. For moral relativist thinkers such as Protagoras, Aristotle and more recently Summer and Mackie, morality is relative to place, time and culture. They find examples within our world and differing societies to support the moral viewpoints".

Above is the conclusion to the full mark answer "explain the concept of relative morality". The conclusion here is strong, and also qualified by words (underlined) such as "however" and "similarly" which are indicators of an attempt to analyse rather than just describe. Notice also the use of examples, and the introduction of authors' names. It is also fully relevant to the question, not deviating into evaluation when it isn't asked for.

How to Structure an Argument

MIND-MAPS

A mind map is a visual and logical representation of a complex set of relationships. It is statement of those relationships rather than an explanation, but it does provide us with a scaffolding on which to hang an argument.

Here is one example of a mindmap on the key ethical theory of Natural Law. It presents us with a way of arguing about this theory. You can use this method and develop it for yourself and try producing your own for areas of the syllabus not discussed in this book. The technique would be the same.

1. Think through what is the starting point. Are there any assumptions the theory makes about the world or human nature.

2. Think through the end or final point of the theory. For example, Kant claims that a world of human beings obeying the categorical imperative will be the best of all possible worlds or summum bonum. What is the relationship between the three Kantian postulates (or **ASSUMPTIONS**) of autonomy (self-rule), immortality and God? Puzzling through this kind of relationship will help you construct a argument about Kant.

3. What are the key steps a philosopher takes to move from assumption to conclusion? Again, using Kant as an example, it is the categorical imperative which really helps us define what is good and gives us the right motive for action - "duty for duty's sake."

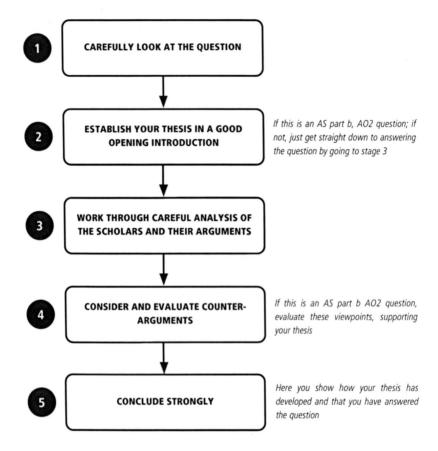

1 CAREFULLY LOOK AT THE QUESTION

2 ESTABLISH YOUR THESIS IN A GOOD OPENING INTRODUCTION

If this is an AS part b, AO2 question; if not, just get straight down to answering the question by going to stage 3

3 WORK THROUGH CAREFUL ANALYSIS OF THE SCHOLARS AND THEIR ARGUMENTS

4 CONSIDER AND EVALUATE COUNTER-ARGUMENTS

If this is an AS part b AO2 question, evaluate these viewpoints, supporting your thesis

5 CONCLUDE STRONGLY

Here you show how your thesis has developed and that you have answered the question

In summary, a mind-map sketches out a skeletal structure and allows us to take a starting point in our analysis. It is a useful memory aid for an exam, and also ensures the essay moves in a logical direction.

Using Natural Law as my example, I take as my starting point the assumption of **SYNDERESIS** in Aquinas' theory, because he states that all human beings have an innate knowledge of first principles (the primary precepts). In general we are born with the desire to "do good and avoid evil."

It might be seen as a starting point because according to Aquinas, we, by our nature, pursue good ends which are rational. These good ends are the primary precepts which lead to personal and social flourishing. So, if we didn't want to do good, we wouldn't want to pursue rational ends.

The primary precepts are then applied to produce secondary precepts. Notice the ones listed are Roman Catholic applications which may be disputed. No secondary precept is absolute, although when we read Catholic documents such as Veritatis Splendor (1995) the secondary principles seem to be presented as absolutes.

We now have a logical structure for any essay.

NATURAL LAW MINDMAP

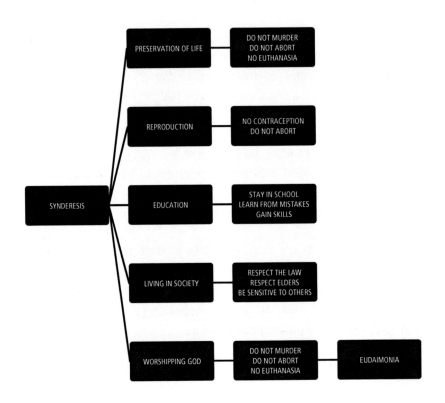

LEGO BLOCKS

We can use lego blocks to build up a scholar's argument where each block represents a key idea. This is just a visualisation of an argument. Those blocks could all be of one colour; however, there could be other blocks that are of a different colour which act as examples the scholar uses at various points throughout their arguments - where would you place those examples in the structure?

Other coloured blocks are the additional points the scholar makes, but you have decided that they are not strictly relevant to the question you are answering at this point. When you look at the tower, do you clearly know and understand what part of the argument the blocks represent? If you do, some potentially good analysis has gone on.

JENGA BLOCKS

This exercise can also be done with Jenga blocks. This enables you to make a link between **ANALYSIS** (A follows from B) and **EVALUATION** (X is stronger than Y). The blocks can be built up, with each block representing a part of a scholar's argument.

A person then has to evaluate the argument that you have built up, and remove a block - that block representing part of the argument the scholar has put forward. If you feel you want to defend that scholar then you can replace that block that has been removed by your interlocutor (a fancy word for the person who is questioning you), if you feel you can say how that scholar would respond to the person making the counter-argument.

You can try to attack an argument at its base, not at the end of the argument where it might have a few less secure sections. Maybe we all have parts of our arguments that are weaker at their fringes but we like to think our main principles are built on more solid ground. But imagine how devastating it would be to attack an argument at its base; the entire Jenga tower falls and the argument has to be built up again.

If you want to attack an argument one effective way of doing so is to attack the base assumptions.

For example, Brian Davies has raised the point that it does not take a God to guarantee Kant's summum bonum - maybe a pantheon of angels could do the same. That might be a valid criticism, but it is attacking the end of Kant's argument and doesn't address the issue of whether Kant is right to suggest that the universe is rational and that the summum bonum has to be in place within such a moral framework.

Exposing Logical Fallacies

The following fallacies or mistakes in logic (things that don't follow) are found in any course of ethics. We can link this to one of our initial objectives to establish the consistency or otherwise of a theory. When considering a philosophical argument, one way of attacking the argument is to expose the mistake or fallacy which underlies the process of reasoning (rather than the foundational assumptions discussed above). We can introduce our exposure with a suitable analytic word "however" or "alternatively."

RESTRICTING THE OPTIONS

If I say "the world is flat or square" I am being forced to choose between two things neither of which are true. Such fallacies are argued even by philosophers (Euthyphro's dilemma and Hume's fork are two examples encountered in ethics).

One philosopher, Rosalind Hursthouse, expresses this fallacy thus:

> *"In some theatres where David Mamet's Oleanna was performed, a noticeboard in the foyer invited those who had seen the play to answer the question, "Who is right? Her or Him?" and thousands of people signed up saying "Her" or "Him." How could they possibly fail to see that the alternatives presented … so signally fail to exhaust the possibilities? Neither was right." (On Virtue Ethics page 45).*

Euthyphro's dilemma, first expressed by Plato, sets up the following conundrum: is something good because God commands it or does God command it because it is good? If goodness is good simply because God commands it, then it appears arbitrary what God commands - we cannot doubt or question God when he orders Joshua to slaughter the inhabitants of Jericho.

If God commands something because it is good then morality is independent of God and God becomes irrelevant to moral questions.

But notice here that there are only two choices. Suppose that a third view is actually the correct one: that God commands things because his character is good, and his character is the ultimate definition of goodness (love, kindness, compassion, mercy)? We are not allowed by Euthyphro's choice of two alternatives to argue for a third possibility: God's commands are good because his character is good. At essence it has nothing to do with what he says.

Slippery Slope

Slippery slope arguments imply that if one thing changes, it will cause a slide into a disastrously bad situation. Of course this could be the case: for example, if we remove all traffic lights people will eventually ignore all traffic signals. But does it have to be?

This possible fallacy exists particularly in the abortion and euthanasia debates. Free up the laws on euthanasia, it is argued, and there will be a general decline in human life. But does this have to be true? Can't clear barriers be put in place to halt the slide or even prevent it ever starting? Is that what the new Starmer guidelines on euthanasia are trying to do: to clarify and define limits? Or the Oregon rules in America?

Exposing this kind of fallacy could form an element of the core of any applied ethics essay.

Analytic or synthetic: confusing the two

The statement "all swans are white" sounds like an analytic statement, true by definition. However the existence of black swans proves that it is actually synthetic, true or false by experience. By presenting it as a self-evident truth we cause people to disbelieve us when we present them with a black swan. In a sense, we close our minds to truth.

In the same way, if we say "God is good" by definition, we close our minds and can explain away the evidence in the world that God is not good (for example, random suffering and the sort of genocide that started in the book of Joshua). If "God is good" is a synthetic statement, then we need to debate the evidence for or against, and sharpen up what we mean by "goodness". We might yet establish God is good, but we will do so on the basis of the evidence, rather than the fraudulent basis of defining him as such.

Correlation does not mean causation

In the empirical world we observe things happening at the same time. Abortion rates rise as sexual morals change, for example. We might infer a causal connection between the two: a change in sexual morals causes a rise in abortion for example. But for this to be valid reasoning, we must establish that all other possible causes of the rise in abortions are not true. For example, poor contraceptive education or lack of availability of contraception or simply that people have access to abortion procedures who did not before. Causal links must be established, in every subject, not least applied ethics.

Circular argument

We have already seen that the ontological argument for the existence of God may be an example of a circular argument. A circular argument begins in one place and ends up in exactly the same place. If I say "goodness is what people desire, people desire happiness, therefore happiness is good," I have ended up exactly where I began, and we're arguably not much wiser about happiness or goodness. Yet this is exactly what Mill argues in his essay on utilitarianism. "No reason can be given why the general happiness is desirable, except that each person, so far as he believes it to be attainable, desires his own happiness."

Another circular argument may be Aristotle's theory of Natural Law, adapted by Aquinas. This is based on the idea that goodness is something observable, defined by the ends or purposes rational people pursue. But this argument appears to end up where it started: "the good is what most rational people pursue, rational people pursue money, therefore money must be good."

Generalising the particular (for example, Mill's proof of utilitarianism)

Bertrand Russell describes this fallacy: "This is the fallacy of thinking that because there is some property common to each of the individuals in the group, this property must apply to the group as a whole. Bertrand Russell (1872-1970) gives an absurd example of this: it is true that every member of the human species has a mother, but it is a fallacy to say our species as a whole must have a mother. In the same way it is true that each one of us as individuals desires our own happiness, but it is a fallacy to say that 'the aggregate of individuals' desires happiness for the aggregate."

Any question on meta-ethics could involve a discussion of the naturalistic fallacy. As the name suggests, this implies a mistake in reasoning. But what if the fallacy is itself a fallacy? For the implication is that we cannot validly move from an "is" statement: "pleasure is good" to an "ought "statement: "you ought to maximise pleasure". Yet this is exactly what many philosophical theories (such as utilitarianism and natural law) do. Are they all wrong to do so?

Here is a meta-ethics question which could employ a detailed analysis and evaluation of this fallacy, and maybe, as an A grade answer, expose the fallacy within the naturalistic fallacy. As with example 1 above, I have added my comments to show the strengths of the essay.

Practical example 6

▸ **"Moral statements are merely an expression of feeling."**
Discuss (OCR June 2011)

*The branch of ethics that discusses the meaning and indeed the
validity of the word good is called Meta-ethics, meaning 'beyond'
ethics lies ethical language. From here there are two separate
branches: cognitive, where "goodness" can be known as an analytic
(Moore), or synthetic (naturalists like Mill). Philosophers divide
between Naturalists, who believe goodness is somehow observable as
some property of the world, and non-naturalist; and cognitive and
non-cognitive, where "goodness" cannot be known as a property of
the world. Within the non-cognitivists are another group called
emotivists, who uphold the view that the word good is merely an
expression of feeling. I partially agree with the emotivists view that
moral statements are merely an expression of feeling, but I also think
that as the 'good is so exceedingly ambiguous' (Stevenson) that any of
the meta-ethical theories have validity to them.*

Excellent opening paragraph, demonstrating the crucial division and
showing that you are taking a clear line on the question. I hope, though,
that this student won't sit on the fence - not a good place to be in this
debate.

*Emotivism says that moral statements merely express positive or
negative feelings; it is mainly based on ...*

better to say "it's an empirical tradition which stems from ..."

... the work of the Scottish philosopher and empiricist Hume and the idea of Hume's fork. "When you pronounce any action or character to be vicious, you mean ... you have a feeling or sentiment of blame."

The student curiously doesn't tell me what the fork actually is - the analytic/synthetic distinction, but it's a very important point nonetheless.

This idea was taken forward by AJ Ayer who also believed that moral statements were primarily expressions of emotion, hence Emotivism, his theory has been called Hurrah-Boo theory.

Why is it called this? Always give a brief explanation.

An example of this is to imagine you and a friend are at a football game supporting different teams. When one team scores you cheer and your friend boos. According to this view, saying 'euthanasia is right' is the same as saying 'Hurrah for euthanasia!'

This is a brilliant analogy because this is exactly what it means.

This is the belief, called logical positivism, that any genuine truth claim must be able to be empirically tested and as moral judgements can't be tested they aren't genuine truth claims and therefore are only expressions of emotion. However, there are a few problems with Ayer's argument. Just because something is morally justifiable, such as abortion, doesn't mean that we passionately support its practice as he suggests in "Hurrah-boo theory" as well as this, this argument is self-refuting. It claims that "Any genuine truth claim must be able to be tested by sense experience." But this claim itself can't be tested by sense experience. So, by its own standard, logical positivism can't be a genuine truth claim.

This is a fascinating point and goes to the heart of the fallacy of composition Ayer and Hume make - it's an either/or fallacy eg "This table is either blue or red" closes off the options. Actually, the table is brown. (See the chapter on fallacies).

> In contrast to the logical positivists and emotivists are duty based ethics, such as Kantian ethics. Kant believed that morality did not rest on sense experience as Hume would suggest but instead ...

Moral maxims are derived (there's a missing phrase, which is why I've interrupted to supply it, so always read your work through).

> ... through a priori reason, as ethical principles aren't empirical like an act utilitarian would state but, instead, are necessary truths for rational beings. Kant not only believed that emotion had no part to play in the meaning of the word "good" but also in the way in which the "good" was brought about. "The good will shines like a jewel for its own sake" - Kant. Kant believed that the absolute moral good derived from the categorical imperative had to be acted out purely out of "duty for duty's sake," we should have no ulterior motive to do good other than it being the right thing to do, emotion contradicts with this virtue. Similarly, divine command theorists would state that what is good is what is commanded by God, and we should follow these laws out of our duty to God's commands. I do not fully agree with the duty based ethics view on morality that it should be purely out of duty, I personally agree more with Hume's assumption that "reason is the slave of the passions" and that the removal ...

The student means "addition", not "removal". Small mistakes do matter because they can suggest to an examiner a confusion and lack of clarity.

... of an emotive force behind our morality makes it more virtuous than purely "duty for duty's sake."

The essay is crying out for a definition and discussion of naturalism here. One of the hardest things to grasp is that Kant who is normally described as a transcendental idealist (a non naturalist) is being redefined by some philosophers (such as Huw Price) as a naturalist who believes in the objective moral law - hard to grasp because it doesn't seem to fit with the idea of the a priori, but does fit with his phenomenal/noumenal categories.

However, another cognitive ethical perspective ...

At last we come back to the main point - I was getting nervous!

... for a moment that contradicts both Kant and Emotivism is Utilitarianism. On face value utilitarianism could seem quite similar to Emotivism or logical positivism as what is morally good is what provides the most pleasure to the greatest number, pleasure being an emotion in most peoples' opinions that is good. However, whereas in Emotivism it is a matter of opinion such as 'hoorah for genocide' - Hitler; for utilitarians the good is derived empirically as you can measure the amount of people who would gain pleasure from an act to those who receive pain. It is also for this reason that it contradicts Kantian ethics as any teleological ethical theory does, as the rightness or wrongness of an action are determined by its consequences rather then the duty behind it ...

Technically the consequences linked to the one intrinsic good of pleasure or happiness.

... but as well as this it's a selfish ethical theory where you act hedonistically and the rights of the minorities can be neglected. However, arguably the good is still derived from feelings, but empirically rather than through opinion. On the other hand, many would argue that there is a difference between what is pleasurable and what is good, for example going out and getting drunk may be pleasurable but is it good?

If you can ask this question then goodness must be independent of the feeling of pleasure, this is Hume's and indeed Ayer's attack on naturalism and in this case Bentham's utilitarianism.

Another branch from meta-ethics is that of prescriptivism. Like Emotivism it is non-cognitive and it agrees that when we make a moral statement we are just expressing our own attitude, but Hare (the founder of prescriptivism) thought that we were also saying that we think other people "ought" to do a the same thing in a similar situation. "This action can be universalisable and so I agree with it and you ought to as well" - Hare. Prescriptivism shows how we can be both free and rational in forming our moral beliefs. Moral beliefs can be free because they express our desires and aren't provable from facts. They can be rational because the logic of "ought" leads to a method of moral reasoning that engages our rational powers to their limits. In this sense, it is very similar to the golden rule, "do as you would be done by."

Yes, what the textbook calls the intrinsic sense of the word good, namely, that it is universalisable.

This rule is a very rational one to follow in ethical thinking as it is relativistic so can cope with special situations unlike absolutist theories such as Kant and his "crazy axeman." But it also means that good is more than just an expression of feeling but an "ought" people should obey in similar situations. In this sense I think that it is a healthy progression from the perhaps idealistic yet unrealistic Kantian ethics.

In conclusion, out of the theories discussed and the ones that I have studied I find prescriptivism most appealing despite the fact that it says that ought judgements are universalisable imperatives, and not truth claims. This leads it to deny the possibility of objective moral knowledge and moral truths which seems to conflict with how we approach ethics in our daily lives. However, unlike emotivism it shows that the word good is more than just an expression of feeling but instead the basis of ethical rules, which gives it more weight as an argument. As well as this, as an ethical theory ...

Doesn't the student mean "as a theory of ethical language that gives space for principles and rules to be rationally debated?"

... where the rules are derived a posteriori there is a more relativistic scope than in Kantian ethics and divine command theory where their absolute rules can lead to immoral outcomes.

Yes. Hare etwas trying to counteract the conclusion that emotivism came to that we cannot have rational moral debate, and Hare is successful in establishing that moral language is language of a certain type, admittedly neither analytic nor descriptive, but meaningful nonetheless.

See Louis Pojman's textbook: "Ethics: Discovering Right and Wrong" (7th edition, 2012) for a brilliant couple of pages on prescriptivism and moral principles.

This is an excellent A* answer because of its clarity, frequent glimpses of real insight, and its well-structured argument (plenty of technical language, names, quotes). But it doesn't quite get full marks for two reasons:

1. The paragraphs on Kant seem to deviate off the moral language point. They didn't need to. The student needed a clear description and definition of naturalism and here an evaluation of the naturalistic fallacy would have been very useful. Most philosophers are naturalists (Mill, Bentham, MacIntyre) at least the ones we study, and naturalism is a very defensible view - make the defence stronger in your analysis. Kant either isn't (traditionally) or is (modern reinterpretations eg Huw Price) a naturalist depending how you argue the case. It is now the emotivists who have gone into retreat.

2. The final paragraph is a little bit weak, I think, especially the last couple of sentences don't do justice to the quality of the preceding writing - a pity, because this student almost nailed this question.

Overall it scored in the exam, 32/35, Grade A*

Evaluating Arguments

Evaluation of the various arguments put forward in the essay is often what differentiates a very good from a good essay. This key skill enables you to move from simply stating what the arguments are in your essay to what you actually think of them. One possible way to start your evaluation is to bring to the examiner's attention the arguments from scholars that have been raised against ones you have outlined.

For example, how does Dawkins argue against the design that Paley suggests is in the world, or, to use Dawkins again, how does his hard materialism act as an evaluation against Christian claims for post-death existence? This is evaluation of an argument using a **COUNTER-ARGUMENT**, and is best used where a scholar makes a direct critique of an argument put forward. Many textbooks are laid out purposefully to encourage you to see how a particular argument works, but also how it has been attacked. But be very aware here: make sure you use counter-arguments to show that you are evaluating the original argument; don't just put forward the counter-argument because you know you are supposed to.

USING TENNIS GAMES TO EVALUATE

The Jenga block game suggested before is a good way of seeing how arguments work against each other, and there are other ideas too. A virtual tennis match between either a single set of players or two scholars on each side (think James and Swinburne vs Freud and Marx on religious experience; imagine Federer and Murray vs Nadal and Djokovic) could see how "points" on each side could be scored.

What if deuce was reached? Would you be able to bring in another scholar, or would you purposely leave the strongest point on each side to the end so that an ace wins that match? I once played tennis in the classroom using a balloon, and it was chaotic fun, with each team trying to create the smash that would win the game. It beats the lists of evaluations that we are all prone to draw up - or at least acts as a supplement to them.

But I don't think that this is enough for a full marks essay, and I think this penultimate point is one that is often missed out in essays.

CRITICAL COMPARISON

Many B or C grade essays have a sense of flow and purpose; the student knows the key components of the scholars' arguments and they have provided some responses to those positions by using, often successfully, counter arguments. The student then concludes by giving some fairly nondescript judgement. Such essays are on the podium and often in the right area but it sometimes surprises the student that they fail to get awarded an A grade.

I would argue that there has been a lack of critical comparison of the strengths and weaknesses of the arguments and the counter-arguments that have been put forward in the essay. Putting forward arguments and counter-arguments alone is not enough. Evaluation of those arguments is needed, and one way that can be carried out is by building on what you have done in evaluation by stating your **PHILOSOPHICAL JUDGEMENT** as to why the strengths of Dawkins outweigh the strengths of Paley or vice versa.

Why do you think that an argument carries greater philosophical merit? Have you uncovered a missing **PREMISE** in one of the arguments? Do you think that a position takes a leap in logic and therefore does not work, and because, you suggest it does not work it cannot be philosophically justified - what about Copleston's contention that "everything within the universe is contingent therefore the universe itself is contingent?" Does this work? Or, for example, do you think James has successfully established the reality of a religious experience, despite the possibility that some of those experiences may have been illusory, as Freud suggests? In revision, we need to think about what we will argue and what arguments we are more philosophically convinced by. It is amazing how many students don't take this step.

If you have been brave in your opening paragraph, you may have indicated the line that you are going to argue, (the **THESIS**), but in that opening you did not state why you were going to go down that route. Critically weigh the arguments up; you have seen how they act against one another and the way they evaluate the **STRENGTHS** and **WEAKNESSES** when they are placed against each other (and, as I say, any good textbook will help you with how the arguments look against each other in evaluation). Now you assess how they critically compare with each other under your philosophical lens (using the personal pronoun "I" if you so wish).

So many essays are ones in which the voice of the student is never heard. What are you going to argue? Don't miss out this crucial stage. It does not really matter where you do it in the essay, but it would seem logical that, after you have seen how the arguments act as evaluations against each other, you add your own robust evaluation through critical comparison of the merits of the arguments you have used in your essay.

REVISION TIP FOR TEACHERS

Set a question with their name in the title. Here's a suggestion: "Discuss Sarah's response to euthanasia." This requires Andrew to put forward his views (possibly using the essay structure suggested above).

Sarah could also write in the first person, and the title becomes "a critical analysis and evaluation of my response to euthanasia." This is a useful exercise for getting students to take centre stage in doing ethics. If we get them used to presenting their argument in extended form, then they should have no problem presenting a shortened version of the same. The lack of a personal argument rather than too much of it is a more common failing in ethics essays.

REVISION TIP FOR STUDENTS

Work in pairs on an essay. Using the title suggested above, and the method outlined in this booklet, write an essay in the following way. John writes the first part of the essay in which he shows the examiner that he knows what the question is asking (about euthanasia, and starts to analyse euthanasia, using various scholars to help him. John then goes on to show what he thinks about euthanasia with a clear and personal evaluation of the main ethical issues she has with it, demonstrating what he thinks are their strengths and weaknesses. For example, what does he think of the often used **SLIPPERY SLOPE** argument? His partner then brings in some critical comparison in response to John's evaluations, noting the strong, weak, valid and invalid arguments that John has raised. John will then get a chance to come back to the point his partner has made, and in this way, some good critical comparison can go on.

A Practical Approach to Essay Writing

Students reading this book may well feel they would like more examples of actual answers which have been either successful or unsuccessful in an exam. The reason why I have not supplied them is that there is a tendency for candidates to think there is one right way of answering a question, or one right style of writing for A grade. This is definitely not the case: let me put it even more strongly - this sort of thinking is a major reason why some candidates fail to get the grade they think they deserve, because they have a pre-programmed response in their minds, and they haven't practised the skill of writing analytically.

In this chapter I will do two things which I hope go part way to satisfying anyone who feels slightly disappointed. First of all, I am going to give two real world examples of essays written under exam conditions (no notes, twenty-five minutes). The first will be an example of an answer that falls short of the analytical skills required for A grade, and the second is an example of an answer that satisfies the criteria for analytical writing I have in mind.

And secondly, I am going to suggest an exercise which you can do for yourself, or with your friends, which my experience suggests will truly build analytical skills, if you're prepared to be disciplined in your attempt to improve.

Example 1: Explain the main principles of classical utilitarianism (OCR May 2013 Q4a)

> *Utilitarianism is a teleological, relativist approach to making moral decisions. The main thought when considering utilitarianism is that consequences are more important than actions and this leads to the thinking that "the end can justify the means." What this is principally saying is that no matter how horrific the act, as long as the outcome produces a better situation it can be claimed to be morally right.*
>
> *This leads to the utilitarian thought of happiness. Utilitarians focus on happiness when making moral decisions and believe that it is highly important for the result of any action to produce the most happiness for the greatest number of people. An example of this would be four policemen who have captured and are holding a prisoner. Now, the terrorist refuses to speak so the police go and get his family and begin to torture them. Under utilitarianism this is justifiable as, although there is suffering for the terrorist and his family, it is reducing the amount of suffering that would be caused if the terrorist attack as planned. So in other words, an act thought to be morally wrong can be justifiably right as long as the outcome produces a greater amount of happiness.*
>
> *Another of the key principles that come from utilitarian thinking is that the individual happiness of people throughout society leads to a happy and prosperous society. This is the thought behind the idea that ends justify means as when there are more*

people happy then society as a whole will work better and be in general a happier place.

However, another form of utilitarianism focuses on personal preferences as well as social preference. This treats all individuals as complete equals meaning that if seven men were captured and only one innocent person who has a cure for cancer was at threat, it would be wrong because the interest of seven outweighs the one.

However, other utilitarian thinkers would claim that harming the seven to save the one would be justifiable as a cure for cancer would save many lives therefore increasing the amount of pleasure to its maximum and justifying the injury of the seven who have captured him.

Overall, the main process of utilitarian thinking is to consider the consequences and not the actions. (376 words)

▸ Evaluation

Before you read my evaluation it might be worth awarding a mark for this answer to a part a question out of 25. How successfully does it answer the question set? How clear is the analysis? Is all of the answer relevant? Remember that examiners only mark positively - in other words they give credit where understanding is demonstrated and do not take marks off for irrelevance or confusion. The key question to ask is this: does the essay select and demonstrate clearly relevant knowledge and understanding through the use of evidence, examples, and analysis relevant to this question?

My evaluation looks like this:

1. Knowledge is limited and only partially accurate. One big deficiency is a failure to address this question throughout, particularly to give content to the idea of "classical utilitarianism". The names Bentham and Mill are never mentioned. So the answer is presented in very general terms, and even then, not very clearly. Notice also how the essay begins with an assertion "utilitarianism is a teleological, relativistic form of ethics" which is never explained or analysed. What exactly makes utilitarianism "relativistic" and what does the term mean?

2. Limited understanding. The idea that classical utilitarians have one idea of intrinsic goodness and apply this as an empirical, measurable test is only hinted at. Nor is the difference between Bentham's hedonic utilitarianism and Mill's rule utilitarianism addressed - you could argue that there are two rather different ways that these two classical utilitarians address the question of what are the most important key principles. Mill adds justice and rights to his concerns, and Bentham doesn't. Mill introduces what later philosophers have called rule utilitarianism, Bentham does not. Mill has a very different view of pleasure as a qualitative idea - they don't agree on the basic meaning of the one intrinsic good.

3. Selection of material is not appropriate. Particularly the very confused and garbled treatment of Singer's preference utilitarianism. This is irrelevant because this is a modern, not a classical, form of utilitarianism, and this should have been clarified at the outset. Moreover, the whole answer is very generalised, and begging for some specific argument from either

or both of the classical utilitarians that are on the syllabus.

4. It addresses the general topic rather than the question directly. This is absolutely what this answer does. It is much too generalised, and then wafts around the terrorist example without ever proceeding to analyse the utilitarian mind, apart from a quite correct emphasis on balancing a calculation of pain and pleasure.

5. Limited use of technical terms. In fact there are very few technical terms in this essay. The candidate manages to avoid mentioning act versus rule considerations, or qualitative versus quantitative pleasure. These terms are in the syllabus. The candidate fails to mention the Greatest Happiness Principle or explain it fully. And although the important concept of equality is hinted at in the paragraph on preference utilitarianism, the candidate never quotes Bentham's famous principle of equality: "everyone to count as one and no-one as more than one." Having never quoted Bentham, the candidate obviously can't unpack what this principle means.

Verdict: a cast iron 7/25 - a level 2 answer which would fail. Which is what the examiner gave it.

Example 2: Explain the main principles of classical utilitarianism.

Classical utilitarianism includes the act utilitarian ethics of Jeremy Bentham and the rule utilitarian ethics of JS Mill. Both share some characteristics and principles, but at the same time, have differences in working out those principles, which are best brought out in contrasting one with the other.

Both Bentham's and Mill's theories share a common telos or goal, which is maximising happiness for the maximum number of people - the greatest happiness principle. This implies an empirical calculation of the greatest good based on adding two maximums: a balance of happiness over misery for the individual and then adding up the number of people involved to get an aggregate.

Underlying this broad, general maximising principle is a principle of intrinsic goodness. Bentham argues that there is only one intrinsic good, pleasure and one intrinsic evil, pain. Mill starts his essay by appearing to agree, but quite rapidly departs from Bentham's view that it is only the quantity of pleasure and pain that matter - the quality or type of pleasure is not relevant. Mill argued that some pleasures were qualitatively superior and so worth more in the calculation: he would include such things as education, reading, and listening to Mozart as higher intellectual pleasures which are superior to eating, drinking and having sex. In this sense the interpretation of this common principle is different.

Bentham also implies that happiness exactly equates to pleasure. As JCC Smart pointed out, it does raise questions about whether it is all that desirable to be hooked up all day to a pleasure machine, passively receiving pleasure stimulus. Mill would agree with this later view that some pleasures were "bad": he saw happiness consisting in many and various pleasures, few and transitory pains, and a predominance of the active over the passive. He went on to add the importance of having right expectations in order to be happy, which seems to suggest he was influenced by the philosopher Aristotle in his working out of what this happiness principle means.

Finally, to the principle of aggregating or maximising goodness, and of pleasure (however defined or qualified) being the one intrinsic good we need to add the principle of equality. Bentham emphasised that "everyone was to count as one and no-one as more than one" and this radicalism places the Queen's happiness as of equal value to my own. Mill would have agreed, but again he goes further. For an individual to be happy it is not enough to make my own individual hedonic calculation of pleasure. There is a social dimension to happiness, and so Mill would add further principles to this equality principle which in Bentham's form is presented in individual terms. He would argue for a strong guarantee of rights and principles of justice as foundations to a utilitarian ethic, because without this kind of social security no individual can be truly happy. This principle is one of the things driving Mill to argue for wise following of certain rules which society has, by experience, shown to benefit utility.

(504 words)

▶ Evaluation

1. The knowledge is accurate and used selectively to build an argument about three underlying principles; the maximising principle, the pleasure principle and the equality principle. It is clear where the answer is heading.

2. The understanding is good, both of the similarities and differences between the two approaches, without descending into evaluation. Mill disagreed with Bentham on a number of points and here the nature of the disagreement is explained in order to clarify the principles.

3. Selection of material is good, with an eye on the clock. It's a little longer (504 words compared with 376, or 25% longer): but then good candidates tend to write faster and use the time more effectively which is why it's essential to practise this skill. I think the first candidate would have written slowly because he or she is very uncertain about where the answer is heading.

4. Technical terms are woven in and accurate. Examples are used but only as very brief illustrations (in contrast with the first answer which repetitively labours one illustration).

5. The issues are engaged with throughly and three principles clearly selected - not too many, nor too few, but enough to present a through answer in 25 minutes. This is why a strategy and selection is so important - plan before you plunge.

Verdict: 25/25 fulfilling the criteria for a level 5 answer, full marks.

BUILDING ANALYTICAL SKILLS

There is an exercise which I often set my students which involves taking two different coloured highlighter pens. You can do this by yourself, or in pairs or as a classroom exercise.

1. Mindful that examiners like the correct use of technical language, the first exercise involves highlighting all uses of technical language in your essay. Try this with the two examples above. How many instances are there of technical language in essay one compared with essay two? Technical language here includes words like "teleological", "hedonic", "relativistic" and "consequentialist", or "act" or "rule" utlitarianism.

2. Having done this, go through each usage and give it a tick if the context suggests a clear and correct usage. Notice, you don't need to define every term, although sometimes you can give a small clue that you know what it means. So in the second essay, the candidate says "goal or telos" - giving the Greek word for the same English term "goal" and in the process demonstrating that the term is understood.

3. Take your second colour highlighter and now highlight every example of analytical words or phrases like "because", "therefore", "in order to." If you're stuck, have a look at my list of analytical words and phrases in the next section. This is not meant to be exhaustive, but identifies the kinds of phrases and words which show you are analysing and not merely asserting.

Now try turning the entire answer into a brief scheme which goes: opening paragraph theme - next paragraph - next paragraph and conclusion. here's how the second answer maps out:

- **PARAGRAPH 1** - Three principles of utilitarianism will be compared and explained in Bentham and Mill's classical forms.

- **PARAGRAPH 2** - The greatest Happiness Principle.

- **PARAGRAPH 3** - The principle of one intrinsic good, pleasure. Quantitative v qualitative.

- **PARAGRAPH 4** - How Mill alters Bentham's hedonic idea.

- **CONCLUSION -** The principle of equality and justice illustrates act versus rule.

Notice how often in my scheme the word "principle" occurs. Why is this? Because the question has that very word in it. Now as a final exercise, underline how many times the first essay uses the word "principle" and then how many times the second essay uses it. I rest my case that it's not so very difficult to go through your own work and check whether you are writing analytical essays.

ANALYTICAL WORDS AND PHRASES

Producing reasons (justifying)

- because
- for this reason
- this is supported by
- this is justified by
- this argument is based on

Probing deeper (underlying)

- this assumes
- underlying this view
- this worldview suggests
- the implications are
- this implies
- from an X perspective

Adding something more (extending)

- furthermore
- finally
- as a result
- consequently
- it follows that
- moreover
- also
- therefore

Placing a counter-point (contrasting)

- however
- on the other hand
- in contrast
- this is directly opposed to
- perhaps (with hesitation)
- possibly (with hesitation)
- maybe (with hesitation)
- although
- but
- compared with

Concluding

- in short
- in conclusion
- to sum up
- I have argued
- it has been established
- the preceding analysis suggests

Practical Examples

In this section we take two more practical examples from students writing under exam conditions, and add our comments and our mark. Two relate to ethics and two to Philosophy of Religion.

We then provide two unmarked essays for you to consider as a classroom exercise, or as revision with a friend.

Practical Example

▸ **Explain how a follower of Kantian ethics might approach the issues surrounding the right to a child. (25) (OCR part a June 2010)**

Kantian ethics is based on Immanuel Kant's views. It is an absolutist approach and assumes that humans are autonomous beings, that they have free will. It also assumes that there is a God, and that virtues and morals are innate, which God provided. The ultimate aim for Kant is the "summum bonum," where people aim to achieve perfection. For Kant to reach the summum bonum you must coincide virtues with moral actions, and you will receive the form of the highest good in the afterlife. Kant believes in a prescriptive "ought implies can." This means that if I ought to help an old lady across the road, I can help the lady across the road.

Here we have a list of points, none of which are very clearly explained, related to one another or related properly to the question. This student has a set of bullet points in front of them, rather than a proper, clear, logical plan.

> *Kantian ethics also follows an imperative, not a hypothetical imperative that relies on something else, for example, "if I want X, do Y", but a categorical imperative. Kant's categorical imperative has three formulations which are: universalisability, this means that everything you do has to be universalised that everyone can do it. The second formulation is "never treat a human as an ends to a mean," this promotes the importance of human life. The third formulation is "live as you live in a Kingdom of Ends".*

The essay could easily have started here, with no loss of marks. Again the key terms need to be properly explained. For example, I'm not sure what a categorical imperative really means, or how it would be applied to solve moral issues surrounding the right to a child. The student should have made clear what these issues might be, as this is so obviously a central part of the question. Notice, too, the garbled attempt to explain the second formulation as "an ends to a mean" - a nonsensical statement which illustrates why you should always check your work through. Kant actually said "treat people not just as a means to an end but always, also as an end in themselves." The "also" is important here.

> *For Kantians they might approach the issues surrounding the right to a child in different ways for different rights, for example, they might categorise it into different categories, IVF and abortion.*

No attempt to discuss or consider what these rights are or how they apply to the issues. Why is abortion part of this question? If it is, the reasoning must be made explicit - such as "the right to a child includes the right not to have a child."

> In Vitro Fertilisation is where an egg gets fertilised outside of the mother's womb and gets input later in to the development stage, commonly known as test tube babies. For IVF the mother has some eggs taken out of her body, and then the father's sperm is made to fertilise artificially. Kantian ethics, from the second formulation of the categorical imperative shows the importance of human life, so making an infertile mother or father be able to have a child is giving the right that parents have. Also for the prescriptive "ought implies can", IVF fits this. For a mother who has fertility problems, to say "I ought to have a baby so I can have a baby."

A very weak attempt to explain "ought implies can," which is really related to the argument for freedom and human responsibility. Again the essay reads like a set of points rather than a structured argument.

> However, in the IVF treatment you have to discard embryos that haven't made the successful fertilisation, also the doctors then choose the healthiest foetus to put back in the mother's body. Not only this, but the IVF treatment is not usually successful the first time so you have to keep using more eggs, who have the possibility of life. As Kant's second formulation of the categorical imperative states "you should never use a person to a means to an end". It is important for Kantians to understand at which point the embryo becomes human life.

At last the essay gets on track, but again rather reduces the mark potential by tagging a really important point on at the end of the paragraph, without integrating it into the argument. The personhood issue has key bearing on the debate, as Kant argues for rational beings not collections of cells, and so would hardly argue for the ethics of a collection of cells without a prior argument about personhood.

> In similar issues Kantians might act similarly to abortion. For even though the mother has the child, she still has the right to abort it. She has the right not to have a child. Kantians would be against abortion, because of the second formulation of the categorical imperative, if you didn't want your child because you could not afford it or you wanted to be without responsibility you are using abortion as a means to an end. Also Kant's formulation shows the great importance of human life. However, if the child was endangering the mother's life then Kantians may have a different view, as it is preventing your death for the birth of potential life.

The above argument assumes child = foetus/embryo, which is the sort of issue the question asks us to discuss. If abortion is relevant here, then it's important to say why. The right to kill a foetus is not quite the same as the right to have a child.

> In conclusion, a mixed approach that Kantians would take towards the right of a child. IVF means the second formulation has mixed approaches as it is making a human life but you are using a potential person as a means to an end.

I'm not clear what a "mixed approach" means - and it's the sort of phrase that doesn't help establish an analysis and clear conclusion. The conclusion doesn't follow from the preceding analysis. Overall the point of the question is missed - what exactly do we mean by a right to a child and how does a Kantian apply the categorical imperative to such issues? These issues might include: personhood, the woman's individual right to choose, the future child's welfare, the sanctity of the human embryo and embryo wastage. It's a much a harder question than this candidate suggests. 14/25.

Practical example

Try marking the next two essays yourself, or in groups. Try splashing red ink over these next two essays. Justify the grade you give.

▸ **"Conscience is the voice of God." Discuss.**

I would have to disagree with this statement as I believe that conscience is not the voice of God, but instead a process of reasoning. Many theists, such as Butler, claim that conscience is the direct voice of God and that we should obey it unquestioningly, whereas others insist that conscience is based in our environment, or perhaps derived from reason.

Butler claims that our conscience is the voice of God, and that it "magisterially exerts itself spontaneously without being consulted," by which he means that our conscience makes instant judgements about right or wrong. Since it comes directly from God, it must be obeyed, and all moral actions should be guided by its authority.

However, I disagree with Butler, mainly from a practical point of view. Firstly, there are of course problems with the idea of an actual "voice," because it is difficult to fathom what exactly this would be like. Generally, the majority of people do not have voices speaking to them directly in their heads, so this "voice" is seemingly not literal. Although, this then leads to the question, if Butler does not mean a literal voice in our heads, what else could a voice in our heads be? Also, there is the problem of differing consciences. In society, we can see many different ideas surrounding moral issues, such as abortion and euthanasia. If conscience was indeed the voice of God, this does not make logical sense since God would surely give the same moral ideas to all of us, thus suggesting a relative conscience. This is supported further by the knowledge that we make mistakes and have regrets in life, for example lying to a friend and later feeling guilty. If conscience were the voice of God, this would surely mean that we cannot make mistakes because our conscience tells us not to do something in the first place.

This would tend to suggest that the conscience has an environmental basis even if it is possible to transcend this. It may be that, as Piaget suggests, conscience is progressive and developmental, which is shown by how children often have to be taught not to do things such as steal toys; they do not yet have a full moral sense. Freud goes further than this to argue that conscience is a construct of the mind, and derives from the guilt of going against one's "ego." For non-religious people, this is a response to externally imposed authority, and for religious people, this is a response to their perceptions of God. These *arguments easily explain the variations between consciences, since we all have different backgrounds and upbringings.*

Nevertheless, I still think that it is possible for reason to transcend environmental impact, as Fromm states in her later, "humanistic" theory. He comes to the conclusion that one's conscience is the voice of our true selves reacting to the voice of internalised commands and authority. This explains where conscience has come from, yet overcomes the problems of variation between the consciences.

Thus, I conclude that conscience is not the voice of God, since the issue of variation between consciences is too strong, but instead is a process of reasoning which transcends environmental impact. I still believe that conscience is very much affected by one's environment, as we can see from cultural differences across the world such as in some American states where the death penalty is still legal. Yet, there must be some sort of process of reasoning since it is not the case that everyone from a certain area has the same morality, and I think it is possible to come to a moral conclusion through reason alone; either way, conscience is not the voice of God.

Practical example: opening paragraphs

It's very important to practise opening paragraphs, but at AS a different technique is needed: you must launch straight into your analysis. Notice how I go straight to the point in these examples, which are actually from the A2 Ethics syllabus. I also try to clarify all terms as early as I can.

▸ **"The weaknesses of virtue ethics outweigh its strengths." Discuss.**

> *Virtue ethics is the ethics of character and the formation of character through the exercise of phronesis or practical wisdom - a skill whose exercise builds right judgement in different situations. Proponents of virtue theory, from Aristotle to MacIntyre, argue that good character precedes right action. The central criticism of this theory, that it fails to guide action, is disputed by virtue theorists such as Rosalind Hursthouse, and the argument of this essay is that the central criticism is a misunderstanding, so the strengths do outweigh the weaknesses, and therefore the above proposition is false.*

▸ **Assess the usefulness of religious ethics as an ethical approach to business.**

> *Christian ethics takes a number of different forms. In this essay I will apply three of these to the issues raised by business, particularly responsibility for the environment, for third world suppliers and for employees. The three approaches include a form of Christian relativism, as proposed by Joseph Fletcher,*

Situation Ethics; the deontological absolutism of Divine Command Theory and the unofficial moral viewpoint of the Catholic Church represented by Natural Law as originating in Aristotelean ethics and developed by Aquinas. What is distinctive about these ethical approaches to business, and how useful are they in practice?

▶ **Critically assess the claim that people are free to make moral decisions.**

Freedom, which is a much cherished belief of many, and a key assumption of Kantian ethics and Aquinas' Natural Law theory, may be an illusion. That is the startling claim of a hard determinist like Ted Honderich, tracing a long history that includes, for example, Thomas Hobbes. However, we do not have to accept the verdict of the hard determinist or the implication that moral responsibility is an empty concept and punishment should solely be for the protection of others. For any claim about free will (either for or against) is metaphysical, beyond proof. Moreover, we can take a third way between the extreme of Kant's metaphysics and Honderich's determinism, that of the Compatibilist David Hume, who argues that for choice to make sense there must be an element of causal determinism, and so freedom requires determinism.

▸ **To what extent are ethical theories helpful when considering the issues surrounding homosexuality?**

In this essay I will contrast the view of psychologists such as Freud and behaviourists such as Skinner with the ethical theories of Natural Law and Situation ethics in order to try and assess which is the more useful approach, the ethical or the scientific. The issues surrounding homosexuality are three: the issue of origin of gender orientation, is it environmental or genetic? Because if it's genetic then the idea of a "wrong" or "sinful" nature is surely refuted? Then there is the issue of conduct - cannot ethics give us general principles of conduct which could be applied to both homosexual and heterosexual behaviour? Finally, I will examine certain assumptions we bring to this issue, for example, the assumption that there is one, universal human nature (which both Kant and Aquinas make). If we change the assumption, then does the ethical conclusion not change with it?

The Night Before The Exam

I have assumed throughout his book that you are an exam candidate, and so I want to write a chapter for you to read the night before the exam, which distills the advice we have been trying to demonstrate here.

Essentially there are two methods of writing essays on Philosophy and Ethics.

METHOD ONE: THE THESIS APPROACH

In this approach, discussed in the first chapter, we state our thesis (conclusion) early in the first paragraph. We then develop the thesis in the body of the essay, illustrating it briefly and intelligently and presenting contrasting views if we so wish, (which we reject with good reasons). The thesis is then restated in a slightly fuller way (to reflect the careful analysis that precedes it) as a conclusion.

We should use this method when we are confident we understand the question and its implications.

METHOD TWO: THE "ASK QUESTIONS ABOUT THE QUESTION" APPROACH

Quite often we may not be very confident about what the question is driving at. If this is the case, then we must adopt the tactic of interrogating the question or asking questions about the question. I suggest we ask three questions and then spend a paragraph answering each one before coming to a conclusion. Each question focuses on one element of the exam question.

We should use this method when we are not fully confident about what the question involves.

An example might help here. Suppose I have a question on ethics which asks:

> *"The ethical issues around abortion cannot be resolved without first resolving the issue of personhood".*

What are the ethical issues surrounding abortion? How and with what ethical tools are these issues resolved? What is meant by the concept of personhood? These three questions (none of which have a single answer), woven into an opening paragraph, give the answer a clear, relevant structure - and the thesis should emerge as we develop our essay. The conclusion is then presented as our own answer to these three questions, perhaps arrived at by contrasting the views of specific philosophers and setting up two ethical theories to see how the idea of personhood is relevant to each.

When you arrive in the exam room, you must follow the steps set out below:

Read every question and highlight key words

Every year candidates make the fundamental error of learning a previous essay off by heart and then regurgitating it in the exam. And every year the examiner complains that candidates did not answer the question. So take a highlighter pen in with you and

1. Highlight all the **TRIGGER** words (like "explain", "to what extent", "discuss"). And then,

2. Highlight any words that are **UNUSUAL** or unexpected.

If the trigger word is **EXPLAIN** it is **NOT ASKING US TO EVALUATE.** Evaluation (strengths, weaknesses, what is good or bad about some idea) always occurs in part b answers at **AS LEVEL**. For example "explain the main principles of classical utilitarianism" has the unusual word "classical" in there. By focusing on this word and highlighting it, you are forced to ask the question "what is classical utilitarianism?" and so there is at least a chance that you will avoid the irrelevance of talking about Peter Singer, who is a modern utilitarian.

But (just to be absolutely clear about this) at **A2 LEVEL** we are expected to interweave analysis and evaluation, and this is made clear by trigger words such as "discuss", "assess" or "to what extent."

Sketch out your thesis/key questions about the question

Always make sure there is some additional loose paper on your desk (put your hand up before the exam starts and request it). Then sketch out quickly your thesis, the main points you need to develop it, and any illustrations you may use. If you are genuinely unsure about the question, don't worry: every other candidate is probably unsure as well. Then use method two and ask three questions about the question and impose your own interpretation on it. You will gain credit by this considered and well-directed line which will then emerge as your answer.

My strong advice would be to practise sequencing ideas before the exam, and to have you own mind-map prepared and memorised which you can quickly sketch on a piece of paper as a memory aid.

Be bold in your answer

It's surprising how many candidates come up with statements such as "there are many arguments for and against the ontological argument, and the issue remains difficult to resolve." This is a form of intellectual cowardice which gains no marks at all. Be bold in what you argue, and try hard to justify your approach with good, solid reasons. It is the quality of the argument which gains credit in philosophical writing, not the conclusion you arrive at. Of course, it essential that the conclusion follows.

Analyse, don't just assert

It is tempting to throw down everything you know about, say, utilitarianism in a series of unconnected assertions.

> "Utilitarianism is teleological, consequentialist and relativistic. It sets up the Greatest Happiness Principle. Utilitarians also believe the end justifies the means."

These are just assertions which are peppered liberally with what we call technical language (that is language no-one in the real world ever uses).

Notice that the above opening few lines demonstrate no understanding and no analytical ability. Instead we should be aiming to write more like this:

"Utilitarianism is a theory of rational desire which holds to one intrinsic good: pleasure or happiness. By the greatest happiness principle utilitarians seek to maximise this good in two ways: they seek to maximise net happiness (happiness minus misery) for the maximum number of people. So it is an aggregating theory, where goodness is added up from individual desires to produce an overall maximum good in which 'everyone counts as one' (Bentham)."

You should avoid phrases like "this famous philosopher" and "this issue has been debated for centuries." Is this true? How would we know? Avoid these kinds of broad, sweeping generalisations.

Illustrate your argument

I remember reading an exam report at University which mentioned that one candidate had been highly commended in an essay on utilitarianism for discussing the case of Captain Oates who, during Scott's doomed Antarctic expedition in 1912, walked out of the storm-bound tent in order to sacrifice himself to save his friends, with the words "I may be gone some considerable time." It's an interesting example because it suggests that a utilitarian could be capable of heroic sacrifice rather than the usual illustration candidates give of torturing a terror suspect to find a bomb location.

Spend a few moments working out which examples you will discuss to illustrate key theories and their application. You can pre-prepare them especially in Ethics.

What is the examiner looking for?

In summary the examiner is looking for three things:

- **RELEVANCE** - every sentence linked to the question set and to your main thesis.

- **COHERENCE** - every sentence and paragraph should "hang together" or cohere. The linkages should be clear as the analysis proceeds.

- **CLARITY** - your style should be clear, and in the context, the philosophical vocabulary you use should be clear. You don't necessarily have to define every technical word, but if it does need a little clarification, you can always use brackets for economy. For example:

"Utilitarianism is a teleological (end-focused) theory combining an idea of intrinsic goodness with a method of assessing that goodness by considering consequences."

Essay Rescue Remedy

1. What is the essay's **THESIS**? Can it be clearly identified in the first paragraph? Can it be stated in a simpler and more straightforward way? If so, re-write the thesis.

2. Based on reading the whole essay, can you identify the **REASONS** you give in support of the thesis or conclusion? You should be able to fill in this blank: "In this essay, I argue that (state the thesis) **BECAUSE** (state the reasons and arguments)."

3. Each **PARAGRAPH** should focus on one main idea **AND** should work to support the thesis. **For each paragraph, identify and write down that main idea AND explain how it helps support the thesis.** If any paragraphs don't do this and/or lack focus, think what can be done to make the paragraphs more focused and organised, as well as strengthen support for the thesis.

   Example: "In the second paragraph I explain ... This paragraph helps support the thesis and/or "make the argument of the essay") because it ...

4. Do I accurately and adequately **PRESENT** and **EXPLAIN** the arguments I discuss? How could the presentation be improved?

5. Do I raise and respond to an **OBJECTION**(s) to the overriding view? How could my response be improved?

6. What questions does my thesis raise? What would someone be confused about? Might a reader ask: "I'm not sure what you

mean here, can you please explain this more clearly?" Are there any problems with **ORGANISATION**? Are the arguments convincing? Are the replies to objections weak?

7. Is the **QUESTION** referred to in the opening paragraph and then discussed in every subsequent paragraph? If I took away the title, could a reader make it up correctly from the analysis?

8. Are there spelling and grammatical errors that I need to **CORRECT**?

9. Does the **CONCLUSION** relate to the opening paragraph and the thread of the analysis? Is it strong or weak?

10. Final considerations: identify and omit all needless sentences and words. Eliminate the passive voice: "it could be argued that" becomes: "here I argue that". Cut out everything that is not immediately **RELEVANT** (and necessary) to support your thesis.

Glossary of Key Terms

- **ASSUMPTION** - something taken as a starting point of a view or argument which is unstated or unproven.

- **CONCEPT** - an important idea.

- **CONCISE** - short, brief.

- **CRITERIA** - what standards you would expect; what questions you would expect to be answered. Notice the singular of criteria (plural) is criterion. "The most important criterion to assess all the criteria is ..."

- **DEDUCTION** - the conclusion or generalisation you come to after looking carefully at all the facts.

- **DEFINE** - requires an answer that explains the precise meaning of a concept. A definition answer will include a definition, probably expanded.

- **DESCRIBE** - requires an answer that says what something is like, how it works and what is essential features are.

- **FACTOR(S)** - the circumstances bringing about a result.

- **FALLACY** - a mistake in an argument whereby the conclusion does not follow from what is stated before. The conclusion is therefore rendered invalid.

- **FUNCTION** - what something does its purpose or activities.

- **IMPLICATIONS** - results that are not obvious, long term, suggested results.

- **IN THE CONTEXT OF** - referring to, inside the subject of

- **LIMITATIONS** - explain where something is not useful or not relevant.

- **PROVE/DISPROVE** - both of these require answers that demonstrate the logical arguments an/or evidence connected with a proposition prove requires the "pro" points, and disprove requires the "contra" points.

- **ROLE** - what part something plays, how it works, especially in co-operation with others.

- **SCOPE** - the area where something acts or has influence.

- **SIGNIFICANCE** - meaning and importance.

- **TENET** - a view which someone holds with justification.

- **THESIS** - a proposition which you are seeking to establish as valid.

- **TRACE** - is found most frequently in historical questions (but not only in History courses); it requires the statement and brief description in logical or chronological order of the stages (steps) in the development of, for example, a theory, a person's life, a process, etc.

Getting More Help

Additional sample essays and advice are available on the PushMe Press website for a fully integrated learning experience. Type the i-pu.sh links into your web browser or scan the QR codes to quickly access more help.

http://i-pu.sh/G9L80H22

Download our free How to Get an A Grade in Ethics App for your phone or tablet and get up-to-date information that accompanies this book and the whole PushMe Press range.

http://ethics.pushmepress.com/download